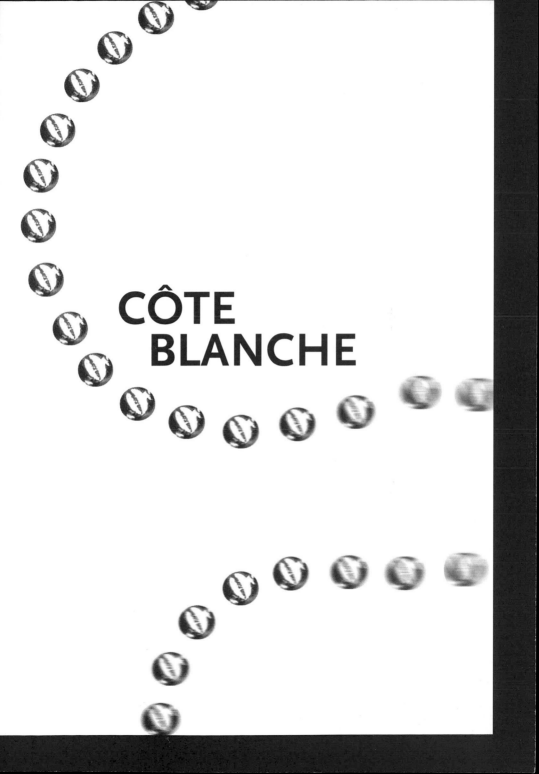

CÔTE
BLANCHE

New Issues Poetry & Prose

Editor	Herbert Scott
Associate Editor	David Dodd Lee
Advisory Editors	Nancy Eimers, Mark Halliday, William Olsen, J. Allyn Rosser
Assistants to the Editor	Rebecca Beech, Derek Pollard, Jonathan Pugh, Marianne E. Swierenga
Assistant Editors	Erik Lesniewski, Lydia Melvin, Adela Najarro, Margaret von Steinen
Editorial Assistants	Jennifer Abbott, Bethany Salgat
Business Manager	Michele McLaughlin
Fiscal Officer	Marilyn Rowe

New Issues Poetry & Prose
The College of Arts and Sciences
Western Michigan University
Kalamazoo, MI 49008

First Edition, 2002.

ISBN	1-930974-18-3 (cloth)
	1-930974-17-5 (paperbound)

Library of Congress Cataloging-in-Publication Data:
Serpas, Martha
Côte Blanche/Martha Serpas
Library of Congress Control Number: 2001132695

Art Direction	Joseph Wingard
Design	Brian Chojnowski
Cover photograph	Patricia McFarlin
Production	Paul Sizer
	The Design Center, Department of Art
	College of Fine Arts
	Western Michigan University
Printing	Courier Corporation

CÔTE BLANCHE

MARTHA SERPAS

FOREWORD BY HAROLD BLOOM

New Issues

WESTERN MICHIGAN UNIVERSITY

for my mother, Nita Cangemi Serpas,
and in grateful memory of my father,
Maurice J. Serpas

Contents

III

Foreword

Though new poets and their poems reach me all but Sundays, only very rarely do they find me (to take a turn from Coleridge). Martha Serpas is, in a highly individual way, a Catholic devotional poet from Louisiana, and she has perfected this, her first book, across fifteen years. Many rereadings persuade me that a double handful of these poems may achieve permanence. Like Elizabeth Bishop, her strong precursor, Martha Serpas practices a severely chastened art of poetry. "St. Charles Crossing" is a subtle tribute to Bishop's "At the Fishhouses" and is appropriately this volume's first poem, after the poignant invocation, "As If There Were Only One." The Augustinian title marks this as a reconversion to life, after the trauma of a beloved father's early death. "God loves each of us as if / there were only one of us" is not an assertion that I believe, but Serpas makes it more urgent for me than I thought it could be. Baruch Spinoza said that we must learn to love God without ever expecting that He would love us in return, but that heals no traumas, though increasingly I believe it to be true.

Elizabeth Bishop's ways of seeing and her self-detachment never quite abandon Serpas, yet the great poet of *North and South, A Cold Spring,* and *Geography III* was a secular artist, who renounced transcendence. Serpas ultimately compels me to associate her with Christina Rossetti, rather than with Bishop or Dickinson. Devotional poetry of high aesthetic quality is difficult to locate in the early twenty-first century. Serpas's, in poems like "Temples" and "St. Joseph, Upside Down and Lost," comes out of the cosmos of Flannery O'Connor, but the temperamental affinity with the poet of *Goblin Market* remains. "Return" is a poem that Christina Rossetti would have understood, as she was expert in what Freud memorably called "the work of mourning."

Serpas's *Côte Blanche* alternately could be titled *The Work of Mourning*. Certain passages in the book are already possessed by my memory, and will not leave me:

> In Louisiana green accuses you,
> spreads like gossip and will not grieve.
> It mats rows of whitewashed tombs,
> small chapels veiled in ivy bloom.

One expects a mystical poet to be an erotic poet also, the two kinds being so close. Serpas's love poems are both heterosexual and lesbian, but she kindles more in the latter, as in the wonderful opening of "In the Garden":

There we are in the Garden:
she a stone's throw away—
my back to fruit trees—
I watch her
        and touch my side.

None of my ribs are missing.
        Her body is her own.

How shrewd the Yahwist,
joining the first lovers with flesh,

with the fierceness

of self-love: the creature craves
a lost bone and tumbles right out of Paradise.

This dark wit juxtaposes two different ways of sexual desire, intimating a reply to critiques calling for "otherness." Serpas's poetry, up to this time, reaches its own wisdom in the final three poems of this volume. "Hell, Late Twentieth Century" takes its starting point from Canto XI of Dante's *Inferno*, the vision of those who suffer for having been "sullen in the sweet air" of God's Creation:

bright fruit we ignored or ate with no taste
sharp winter days we groped past, or slept
through, and that retriever who chased

us from bed to bath, carrying
ball then bone in adoration—we reach
into yellow vapor, touch nothing,
and scratch the air of her head and ears.

I am moved almost to tears by this, though the particulars are not my own, but all of us have wept when we might have been joyous.

As befits an Augustinian mystic, Serpas is strongest in her poem on "Conversion," though her immediate reference is the movement of resurrection from mourning to more life:

But then, to the right of the road,
the shoulder leapt with sunflowers,
the blue sky dangled like a scarf,

And the part of me that was buried
came back like the dead after hard rain,
just pushed up the glass lid

And stepped onto solid ground. Backwater rises
to its own schedule, covers the highways,
you can't tell the bayou's banks

From the road's edge, and then there's no question
of staving off conversion.
Even the dead won't be held down.

The bayou, all through this book, has intimated a freshening of existence.
In the final poem, "Finishing Touch," dedicated to her lover, Serpas extends her
mastery of her art. I hear an overtone of James Merrill in:

I know this,
and still I have to ask for reprieve

in illusion, to linger in this present
flesh, believe in her finishing touch.

The allusion, to an erotic master, is raised to transcendence, since, as
always, Serpas is her own highly original kind of Catholic mystical celebrant.
The poem is governed by Michelangelo's vision, on the Sistine ceiling, of God
creating Adam, and dares to compound erotic and Divine finishing touch:

Each hand found
more skillful than the last, each imprint closer

to Your transforming seal.

A sense of something freshly molded lingers in Martha Serpas's lyricism. I
am moved to prophesy a considerable poetic development for her.

—Harold Bloom

Acknowledgments

Poems in this collection originally appeared, often in different forms, in the following publications:

A Carolina Literary Companion: "'Louisiana Saturday Night,'" "Sex Education"

Ark: "Margin Lines," "Postcard to My Mother"

Columbia: A Magazine of Poetry and Prose: "M Is for the Many," "Chase"

Image: A Journal of the Arts and Religion: "As If There Were Only One," "Little Lake," "Hell, Late Twentieth Century"

Kalliope: A Journal of Women's Art: "Before Ash Wednesday"

Southern Poetry Review: "Port Fourchon," "St. Charles Crossing"

Tar River Poetry: "Southern Women," *"Grand Bois"*

Western Humanities Review: "Finishing Touch," "Elegy," "Day of the Dead, 1996"

Uncommonplace: An Anthology of Contemporary Louisiana Poets (Louisiana State University Press): "I'll Try to Tell You What I Know," "Southern Women," "M Is for the Many"

My appreciation to the Cultural Arts Council of Houston and Harris County for a crucial fellowship awarded during the shaping of this book. I am grateful also to a number of generous teachers for their guidance: Sandra Alcosser, Edward Hirsch, Richard Howard, and Cynthia Macdonald. Thanks to those who read early versions of this collection: Sharon Bryan, Ann Keniston, Molly Peacock, and, especially, Lisa Rhoades. I am beholden to Audrey Colombe for many years of friendship and support.

As If There Were Only One

In the morning God pulled me onto the porch,
a rain-washed gray and brilliant shore.

I sat in my orange pajamas and waited.
God said, "Look at the tree." And I did.

Its leaves were newly yellow and green,
slick and bright, and so alive it hurt

to take the colors in. My pupils grew
hungry and wide against my will.

God said, "Listen to the tree."
And I did. It said, "Live!"

And it opened itself wider, not with desire,
but the way I imagine a surgeon spreads

the ribs of a patient in distress and rubs
her paralyzed heart, only this tree parted

its own limbs toward the sky—I was the light in that sky.
I reached in to the thick, sweet core

and I lifted it to my mouth and held it there
for a long time until I tasted the word

tree (because I had forgotten its name).
Then I said my own name twice softly.

Augustine said, *God loves each of us as if
there were only one of us,* but I hadn't believed him.

And God put me down on the steps with my coffee
and my cigarettes. And, although I still

could not eat nor sleep, that evening
and that morning were my first day back.

13

I

St. Charles Crossing

1.
It is fire that brings me home.
In October the flames start deep
in the cane, the only red and gold
here of autumn; oak and bald
cypress refuse to change color.
And again at Christmas along the levee
cone-shaped bonfires light the river
into a blazing runway. I cannot resist
the bayou's highway, huge mangers
crawling between the smolder and slow water.

2.
My father's cane knife has rusted
a deep color like wine. Its sound
hasn't changed, a metronomic chop
outside the canebrake. No farmer,
he hacks at crabgrass on weekends.
I can feel his heart's bent spine,
belonging and not belonging.
When I was nine, I chewed sugar
with a native oysterman. His quick knife
pressed the pulp into his thumb,
lined hard from opening shells.
      Later, I learned the Valentine
mill and putrid smoke,
how paper flows from what's left:
no syrup ever tasted as sweet.

3.
The bayou widens and curves
toward the Gulf. At the crossing
it's only a thread pulled

from the river. The farther it strays,
the more land it demands,
as if leaving granted all possibility.
     The tracks never arrive,
never part, and even they
were cast off, ten miles from town.
When the trains still ran,
everything must have stopped
for them but the slashes of smoke
and the slow confident stream.

Picayunes

Each year a row of tomatoes disappears,
one less row of coffee cans bracing
loose vines, the new stalks bow-tied to sticks
with old sheets. The old men hardly fish
anymore—skiff and busted Evinrude
trailered on blocks behind an eggshell Ford

that never moves. Once my great uncle
held each proud tomato in his hand, wrinkling
its waxy skin with the fat of his thumb
and counting each bird-peck a casualty
in his war against loss. With a Daisy
pellet gun, he picked off blackbirds, one

by one. His eyes were marlin blue, and the skin
slung from his jaws, maroon as
the concave pack of Picayunes he pulled
from his vest pocket. *Why does God take
the young before the old?* he'd ask, as each
growing season closed, left him awake and alone.

Why do we all, young and old, recite regrets
like morning offerings, like prayer cards stuck
to the mirror's corner—more for comfort
than prompting? Prayers unanswered
many years curl, yellow, and turn rote.
He confesses nothing, counts his losses

like beads: a wife to childbirth, a son
at two years, round face flushed from the south-
eastern sun. For days silent nieces
walked his stroller up and down the block.
He loved his own family bitterly after that,
as if they wouldn't let him loose from his roots.

You learn to stay where you're planted
and save flighty dreams for the old. One
loves one's own bitterly after that—
one clings to them like revenge, like a blight.
A sister washed fruit, cleaned fish, and last,
slid him in the tomb where his brothers are laid

and where she will lie when she lets go
the bitter love that ties her now
to the house with the Ford in the yard,
the boat keeping rain and the fig tree,
ancient and shriveled, like the one Christ cursed,
made black and barren, and never forgave.

Sex Education

I unload boxes from my sapphire
Cutlass. It is Christmas.
The sky furls, waterlogged
wind rattles the chain-link
fence between us. It could be
a tropical storm, maybe a Betsy.

Your dog does not greet me,
his flanks collapsed, thin
fur peeled from his back. A suit coat,
stretched like a pelt, rots on a rack.
The bare slats of your porch
lean into one another as trucks
pound the bridge overhead. Your marsh yard
shrinks with every passing barge.

You send your daughter
out to me, for the basket
of bread and rice and meat.
You are as old as the swamp,
moss and roots, slow
as a mudbug. She throws you
a bar of soap, and you rub it,
wrapper on, across your wide
stomach, below your duster
down your coarse, gray legs.

A mule scratches its ass against
the fallen cistern. Young boys,
river rats licked greasy dark,
carry the groceries inside.
Other children jump like fleas
down the steps—sullen, identical.

I know your story, as
if you told me first-hand:
I teach my boys at home. They'd went off
with whores if I don't. I kept 'em home safe.

Lightning reaches down,
a decrepit finger from the sky.
Tell you mama and you daddy Merry Christmas,
the daughter (sister) calls.

When you walk to church,
the congregation parts
like the Red Sea, forms a perfect
halo around where you sit.

Port Fourchon

They make love everywhere,
atop damp, redwood tables
in Oakridge Park, inside
vacant rooms at the Shady Inn,
in public restrooms, in the bilge
water of his father's skiff,
on the hard-coiled seat
of his '74 Chevy pickup
while he drives.

He wins her love shooting pool
at C.J.'s Friendly Lounge.
Crushing a cigarette with
a steel toe, he stares her down
over the tip of his cue.

He works seven-and-seven,
leaves his truck with a buddy
who got laid off. She sits
in the hazy dusk of the swamp
and peels shrimp on the porch
with her mother, who says,
he works hard, him,
turns her salty fingers,
wipes her forehead with her wrist,
and pulls the long black vein
from the next tiny shrimp.
She wraps the peelings,
their breathless pink color,
tightly in newspaper to deter
foraging cats.

23

When she can get a ride,
she waits for him at the dock.
The deckhands catcall
and they make love between
the cabin top and the Gulf gray sky.

Twelve days, he does not
come off the boat. She
walks to the clinic herself,
the heel of her palm
pressed into her stomach.
Later, she repeats the word,
fetus, a chant, a vein,
another part that cannot be saved.

The Bridgetender

Half past midnight. The bridgetender stands
     on the walkway of the pontoon bridge
counting stars and drinking beer. With his good
arm, he is holding the pony bottle
     against the guard rail. With his stump he is
tapping out a slow count against his ribs.
     The fog sets in, the cars rock by. Three
white-framed houses back, nothing but trees.
Trees and heat and fog stick like cobwebs

And soften like young hair against the face
     of a deckhand whose trawler rounds the bend.
Inside the awkward little house, beside
the controls are a pocket radio,
     lantern, tool belt, and an oyster
knife. A deep horn blasts three times. The tender
     lowers the barriers and flips on
flashing red lights. Two cars and a pickup
bolt through. He halts pulley three and lets them

off the other side. He considers this
     a gift, as if he'd ferried them across
the bayou on his back. Here this is
his portion, and he keeps his words few.
     The cables groan, and the floating bridge,
the little house, and he swing to the west.
     Half in fog and half in red glare, he sees
the *Lady of Fatima* out of Houma
churning past. The deckhand, all of fourteen,

stares at the Airstream waiting at the gate,
     then at the old man's head sticking out
of the little house, out of a worn and stained T-shirt.
He touches his forearm gingerly, runs
     his finger over a swollen tattoo,
its heavy black line a barrier
     between his arm and the blue-gray shadows
of panther claws that tear through his skin.
Even in the red glow the ink looks new.

First

1.

    the oyster grass gathers
around the bow, then the white housefronts,
a saving wash across the shore.
Porches where grandmothers
shell pecans and watch children
ferry the bayou to school. *Au revoir,*
but they do not answer, their language
beaten out of them.

History thickens like warm
air on a June night. At sixteen

We sat on Claude LeBlanc's
dead uncle's front porch and drank to ourselves.
    I drove my Buick right up the lawn,
as if I could will myself into that grave beginning,
or smash it, like a lovebug, against the grill.

2.
I was born, late one season,
in a blue tin clinic, Our Lady
of the Sea. My mother slept—
or tried to. A jaundiced barmaid
played chank-a-chank music on the ward,
while her boyfriend chain-smoked.
I was somewhere, quiet.

During Betsy I was in the womb.
By Camille, just out. By Carmen
I knew what *native* meant
and that my father was not.

3.
The boys' side, the south side, at Holy Rosary—
damp and mysterious—had the ball field
and most of the swings.
Sometimes I walked to the end
of the north's covered sidewalk and watched
their khaki figures flung across the grass.

Under the silktrees I told myself
I was a character in a bedtime story.
I'd forget my name, then remember,
the field blurring into pink mimosa
blossoms and flat bean pods.

After morning rain the road
steamed like dark roast coffee.

4.
At Mardi Gras he wore a large
translucent mask, black eyeglasses
strapped across the nose, and rode
with all the other fathers,
Krewe of Neptune, Float 28.
I stood on the car hood and waved.

Beads by the gross
rained all over me.

5.
One night I was driven out of a pool hall
two-hundred yards
from the house I grew up in,
tossed out like an outsider—a *Texian*.
Exile at least claims a severed belonging.

In my mind he leaves
quietly, stops among the oyster-shells
to wipe dust from his soles—
he is the eye of my storm—
as I brandish my cue, a crusader
just landed on the white coast
of a fearful new world.

6.
Since I was born I have felt the earth
pulling away toward
a white coast of brilliant foam
and sand, gleaming not with some
great absence, but with the fusion
of all possibilities, radiant without color:
wild marsh and oyster grass on a trackless
path for a roustabout God.

Tattoo

She knows being chosen means to choose herself
and seals upon her breasts the Sacred Heart—
a thorn-bound garnet against open lilies,
a pink-and-white ink triptych on her chest.

Every shadow, a creed professed by lines
from votive needles to her deepest cells.
Her body gives life to art, reflects the fade
of dying flesh, and honors God's design.

No second thoughts, she thinks that pain
is easily a choice we make ourselves,
as is admiring her canvas skin
as it ages. Affirmed with words spelled

on a defiant ribbon across her chest,
her blazón: *Even the blackest sheep are blessed.*

In Praise of the Passion Mark

First the unintentional: raspberry
blush, many-speckled lights,
and the message: *oops, sorry.*

Then the hard mark of the all-nighter,
a true Hoover, a hole black as leather
daring you to plummet.

We were dancing, it just happened,
she said, helplessly sentenced
to a week of turtlenecks

in May, in the sticky South. The frozen
spoon failing, she took a curling iron
to her neck and still her mother knew

the mix of teeth and lips and love.
Alone, she admired her shoulder's
violet smear: she was wanted

and had wanted. She'd have it
needled and inked, a permanent
badge of desire, a license for love.

And when the plaid-clad chem teacher
appeared with his bright bruise,
news traveled fast: wanting

does not die after all, after age,
one sort of taking in does not
supersede another. Go

for the jugular. We cannot
be sucked
dry.

Temples

Where the bayou breaks into marshland
And steel bridges join one foothold
To another, the flat-topped shrimpsheds
And rust-pocked ice plants of Leeville

Begin. Huge blocks of ice-blue
And silver jeweled displays slide over-
Head and down the open bellies
Of trawlers sloped below.

Along the planks, hard-skinned hands
Count heads per pound and wade calf-
Deep in brine and shells that spill
From the pans of unquestioned scales.

Sometimes three generations
Work one deck of black mahogany
And wax the grain till it shows
Banks of clouds like glass. A boat like that

Floats on the thought of waves,
Is cause for thanks, like a season
Passed with no storm—nor worse—
That captain knows, who built his little church

On blocks and shells beside the one
Road to Caminada Bay.
Black-shuttered doors flung wide, the white
Frame no more than six feet square.

A son had gone to Viet Nam and
Gone he stayed. The shrine
Has room inside for one
Alone to pray.

Those who come find some companion
In languishing flowers or
Votive tapers, some resolve
In the hum of a half-learned hymn

To take them past temptations.
Outside the booth, beyond
Salt-battered graves losing ground,
Stripped of bricks, now stacked and crumbled,

A house faces the wooden cross,
Sits high on pilings driven deep
Into the marsh. A sign declares
(In red): *Maison d'Imports.*

The captain's wife minds the cash,
Straightens the wall of slick flesh,
Shrink-wrapped bodies, young and fresh,
An adoring host for offer.

Above, a sign: *$1 browsing
(With purchase, free)*. Her silver-
Blue hair catches the light, rising
From the case of hard-core porn.

On the counter she snuffs a red
Scented cone, ignores devoted eyes,
Inchoate stares. She bags roach clips,
Dildos, and leather whips with the same

Blank air, while pilgrims outside
Climb the thirty iron stairs.
Like sentinels at the gate,
The shrines face, rather blasé,

The calling they share. Just
Past Leeville and before Chenière,
Variations of witness are raised,
Two temples of glory and of praise.

I'll Try to Tell You What I Know

Sometimes it's so hot the thistle bends
to the morning dew and the limbs of trees
seem so weighted they won't hold up moss
anymore. The women sit and swell
with the backwash of old family pain
and won't leave the house to walk across
the neighbor's yard. One man takes up a shotgun
over the shit hosed from a pen of dogs.
One boy takes a fist of rings and slams the face
of a kid throwing shells at his car.
That shiny car is all the love his father
has to give. And his mother cooks
the best shrimp étouffée and every day
smokes three packs down to their mustard-colored ends.

One night the finest woman I ever
knew pulled a cocktail waitress by the hair
out of the backseat of her husband's new
Eldorado Cadillac and knocked her
down between the cars at the Queen Bee Lounge.
She drove the man slumped and snoring with his hand
in his pants home and not a word was said.
I'll try to tell you what I know
about people who love each other
and the fear of losing that cuts a path
as wide as a tropical storm through the marsh
and gets closer each year
to falling at the foot of your door.

Little Lake

You could have warned me, Daddy, or I could have asked
    about middle-aged men and whiskey and guns,
about uncut hunting dogs, dead animals, duck blinds
      thick with deceiving reeds. I rode out stupid to the swamp,
to Little Lake with Laurie Lynn, her grandpa, and his friends.

There was wonder to it at first: the flat marsh, thrushes and knees,
    Laurie's pirogue skimming the greasy surface of the lake.
      A deer trailed *us*,
stamping the tread of our Keds into cloven bowls. We circled
    the muddy tracks and ran right into the pursuing men.
They handed Laurie a 4-10—the Labs had treed a coon

so high I could barely see. She fired, and he fell at our feet
    on his back, a red spot like a shaving nick between his eyes.
The dogs dragged a half-drowned muskrat to shore: I aimed and
        shot,
    an ache under my right shoulder and a throbbing
beneath my left. When I missed, they laughed. Bug-bitten

and dirty, I pushed through sharp reeds to the house.
    Nero, never a sire and caged too long, broke loose,
humped me down into wet clover, a vacant look in his eyes.
    As Laurie pulled him off by his collar, I stared at my shorts,
rubbed green smears off their torn hems. Long dark outside,

we lay awake in our bunks and listened to the live sounds of the land,
    rising growls of the hunters. *You raisin'? You ain't got jack
shit! Let's see wha'cha got dere, chu!* When they called me out,
    one reached for my wrist, and, thick with whiskey, said,
You know, cher, the Catholic Church is just a big business, as he ran
      a wide moral

eye up my legs. I had teased Laurie: "a damn Southern Baptist
    and a Republican," but we were still best friends. Best
        friends.
Didn't everybody think like Laurie and me? You did.
    You never said a cross word about anyone:
All beliefs were just to you. All men were just like you.

Tilt

"Hold on with both hands," he said, as he slammed
the gold bar across my seat. I obeyed—
I trusted all men: the pest control man,
bus driver, my teachers. The gray

T-shirt stretched across his belly
left a white skirt over the loops
of his pants. His stubby hands tested well
the locks to my left and right, and then we flew.

Guardrails and strung lights disappeared into screams.
Pride kept my stomach in a tight fist below
my ribs, until the air slowed to a stale stream.
He looked away to the next car that slowed

as he freed me from the seat. I noticed
my mistake as I climbed out—"Tilt-A-Whirl,"
not "World"—although the irony I missed
inched toward me. I curled

my feet into the slime, away from
something close to fear wrapping its hands
around the lever of my wild ride. Ahead, some
bright colors. As soon as I could, I ran.

Grand Bois

South Lafourche High School, 1983

In twelve minutes we could drive the shortcut—
Bayou Lafourche toward Grand Caillou—
My high school friends in an econo Ford.

We saved—more than time, holding our eyes
On the trailing center line—ourselves
From the futures chasing us down. Once

We blew a curve and dived into the marsh.
I saw then what I see now: the young dead
Along the tidewash—miles short of their true ends—

Straying from us, their backs turned,
Their shoulders verging into the haze.
Above the treeline their names—some were friends,

Some were bodies in the halls. Rows of faces,
Rows of cane, the narrow curves and arched moss—
Time we saved, forgot, then lost.

II

Southern Women

Southern women won't shake your hand
when you meet them, my friend says,
they nod while their husbands

squeeze your palm and slap your shoulder.
We walk toward the mausoleum
toward bodies above ground, here land

covers sea water like algae.
I think of the women
I grew up with, kissed in greeting

in the vestibule of Sacred Heart.
Women in veils and without,
with rosaries and novenas,

sometimes with men, but
always with children, and always
when the congregation stands

before a dark space in the wall
of rose marble markers, and the Knights
have lifted their plumed hats

back on their smooth gray heads,
and Father has closed the book,
slid the colored ribbons in place, and

the gallant sword has been handed,
the flag folded in its tight triangle,
it is the women who turn first,

wives and daughters,
into the sun or into the rain,
their heels marring the soft black ground,

sometimes sinking, and whatever season,
they look into magnolia or oak
or wild azalea, something alive,

and the men, brothers, sons
lay down their frozen boutonniéres
and follow.

Chase

When my cat is afraid,
her eyes round into two
coal bearings. She rolls under the hope
chest, skitters across the floor
of the rag wool rug. Her heart
storms behind her silver ribs. I feel
kinks in her stripes as I lie
prostrate, penitent across the bed,
trying to steady her. I don't
know why I chase her, it's not
play, but when I've got her
backed between the white chest
and the sanitized-white
wall, focus all on her wild cheeks
and straight ears, it's my mother's
half-crazed look, nerves popping
like downed power lines, hair hot
as solder, blown back by a fury
I could not understand, now here
before me—terror, cornered
and recoiling just like her.

St. Joseph, Upside Down and Lost

Her hand in her mother's hand,
she walked from the white house
on Green Street to the corner
then down the boulevard to Saint
Mary's. Matching *mantillas* and small
beaded purses clasped in gold, just big enough

for tissue, rosary, and enough
picture prayer cards to handle
any spiritual emergency in the small
time between Mass and dinner at the house.
She learned to pray to her patron saint
and tucked herself into the varnished corner

of a side pew. When you feel cornered,
she was warned, and you've had enough,
turn your heart to your special saint.
Or rather, she discovered, better to hand
your problems to the one in God's house
who can best address your small,

but pressing concerns. For the smallest
of favors, for example, Saint Ann in your corner
is best. To retrieve a lost household
item, Saint Anthony's intercession is enough.
For the seemingly impossible, hand
your petition by way of novena to Saint

Jude. He became her favorite saint,
as none of her causes were small.
Jude, patron of the hopeless, of hand-
wringers, those backed into a corner
by life. And his help was enough
until, grown up, she tried to sell her house.

The *For Sale* sign sat near her house-
front, crabgrass opened around the picket. *Saint
Joseph alone*, she was told, *has enough
pull to grant your wish.* She buried a small
statue in the proper position, cornered
pedestal up. She dug with her hands

but not fast enough to find him when the house
was sold. Saint Joseph, handsome and lost
in a corner of what used to be her very small world.

La Toussaint, 1944

As if it were an old grave, she scrubs his cross
whiter, frees the mortar and his nameplate from the gray

skein of mildew, has her children pull weeds,
find the hollow homes of fallen tomb bricks

at their bare feet. Each holds a flower
for his father, and when their mother slides

the lead cover aside, they see his stern gaze
in the ashen oval photograph. They

crowd on the narrow step, as quickly turn away.
He is, and he is not, in the whitewashed box.

Like most good Italians, he tried to raise
his children along American lines,

the paper read. It should be a joke,
that his children can't swim—barred

from the KC pool with those more
Italian than Columbus or the Pope.

As her children push each carnation's stem
into the vase, she thinks of her grocer, now

part of the communion of saints
until the resurrection of his body

and the mending of the worlds of sin,
worlds without end, without end. Amen.

Return

Voices at the door. Another pot
of gumbo, sausage from Mrs. Terrebonne,
roast beef from a Verret. Keep a list.
Scald dishes, glad for the feel of water
reddening your hands. Eat: chew, then swallow.

A day comes. You remember to be hungry.
You remember to cook. You return

pots, pans, casseroles to the women whose
names are written on freezer tape across
scorched porcelain and copper bottoms. Things
belong to people who belong to earth
and the dead belong wherever they are,

in the places their names are marked.
Thank these women for reminding you.

"Louisiana Saturday Night"

"Louisiana Saturday Night" blares through the half-
opened window of the carpenters' truck.
They crawfish down the tar-papered roof,
harnesses smacking their faded blue thighs.
The dust and two-by-fours of the new
Spiritual Life Center creep
right up to the mausoleum, blocking view
of the Sacred Heart. Once you could see
Him from the main road, now He appears only
over the shell drive, wedged between the wooden
frame and the graves. From this square
of St. Augustine grass, He's chest-deep
in colorless sky, His eyes bored
a good two inches into white marble.

As a kid I'd have blown an ant pile
this size, riddled it with lit
firecrackers like birthday candles.
One red ant digs into the clay
and pushes out dirt its own size.
A woman tends poinsettias
in front of me. I'm sitting
in her shadow. She's watered them
twice, has propped an old tomb
brick against the green-foiled pot.
The leaves flash color between her fingers.
She tousles and fluffs them like pillows,
as if the man behind the marble plate
could feel her there, stroking
temple to hairline, temple
to hairline.

Proof

I stare right at the camera and wrap
My legs and arms around my father,

Who looks at a spot on the auditorium
Floor somewhere between the photographer and

My mother, with the kind of peripheral vision
I learned at Grand Coteau basketball camp

Six summers in a row. One eye on the ball, one eye
On your "man," foot on the baseline, palms up,

Knees bent, weight on the balls of your feet, prepared
For the steal. If my father was on guard even then,

It's no wonder his heart gave out. But his smile *seems* relaxed
Through the salt-n-pepper scruff my mother swore

She'd scrape off herself when the beard
Growing contest at Sacred Heart was done.

My hair is at its longest, too, swipes
My shoulders, like a deflected touch.

Blown up bigger than a glossy 3x5,
This remnant blurs into lint, into a fiction.

M Is for the Many

I touched him more than is appropriate.
His mouse-brown hair downy without Vitalis,
his taut finger around the beads,
an orange fleck of mercurochrome
upon the nail-edge where he'd pierced it
on the front holly. Will Jesus
tend his cuts now, Jesus
worn faceless in the pinch
of his praying hands? My sister

showed our mother a place
between his arm and right ribs,
inside the crook of his elbow
where he still felt warm.
She tells me his hands will cross
this way for the fifty years
of his coffin's airtight guarantee.
Long after our hair grays
at the temples and the soft skin
folds above the bones of our hands,
his lids and mouth will be fixed
in hard curves of makeup around his jaw.

This is not sad,
as at the cemetery after the tomb
was blessed and the ushers
slid the long oak box in, the bus driver
asked to sing a song
for his dead friend's mother.
No one told him it was not proper.
He clasped his hands before him.
M is for the many
things she gives me, he began
to the clear sun and with him
was laughter and mouthing of the words.

Elegy

My father left the door ajar as he
passed between the bedroom and his bath.
I gazed, transfixed, into that eye-width
of light between jamb and frame: a glory
of white porcelain, gleaming tiles, his naked
chest, his penis immersed in murky water,
masked by a swarm of aging hair.

My mother (my lover?) pressed sudden hands
on my shoulders, fixing my heels to
hard wood. But I would not turn away
from light narrowing, ribbon to strand,
and then, out of blue darkness, a thread
cut across my mind, then snapped.

Day of the Dead, 1996

Tonight, in the next state, my mother rests,
propped against pillows in her darkened
bedroom and listens to trick-or-treaters
ring her front bell once or twice; sometimes
the desperate press three times. *I'm not
fooling with all that anymore,* she tells me

on the phone. She does not respond
when the dead visit her, dragging wet leaves,
shoelaces, trailing sheet corners down
her drive. I imagine it pleases her
to make them wait: shuffling feet, glowing
jack-o'-lanterns, whitened skin and bloody eyes.

The youngest wear the sinister faces
of her mortality, masked by over-
flowing energy. The dead leave empty-handed.
She'll meet them in her own time—tomorrow:
her dead—her parents, grandparents,
my father—and the dead of her dead—

those without first kin to bring flowers,
scrub tomb bricks, say prayers. After morning
Mass she'll walk out to greet them, take stock
of her own uncarved marble, as Father
blesses their mildewed tombs, carnations frame
the bedsides of her encroaching dead.

Postcard to My Mother

from the Berkshires

I saw a woman place flowers at a grave:
her body wrapped tight in navy wool, her hands
willful, the knuckles raised to yellow peaks
around the stems—the only shock
of color in the Lenox winter wood.
    These trees have set their minds against leaving—
she must be comforted that Spring comes for no one.
    In Louisiana green accuses you,
spreads like gossip and will not grieve.
It mats rows of whitewashed tombs,
small chapels veiled in ivy bloom.
Believe this: she saw her love
lowered inside the frozen earth,
jarring the land and its seasons.
Our dead never break ground. They wait
in marble kilns, safe and kitchen-warm.

Last Turns

Houston, Texas

The Gulf Coast's first female Southern Baptist
pastor, auburn hair and full-length mink
shimmering in the morning light, shovels dirt
from a bulldozer's blade into her husband's grave.

The mourners check their watches, and behind her
a stern voice says, *I hope they get 'im put away
before it rains.* As they shuffle off to cars,
she nods. Workers roll aside the canopy,

fold the slip-covered chairs into carts,
peel away the layers of that phony astroturf
from damp ground waiting—she knew all along—
underneath. Giant machines jerk the vault

free of supports and lower the molded copper
lid onto its mate. Among dark green easels,
carnations, and mums, a boy machetes sod
and fits the pieces in perfect calendar

squares across the plot. Every morning
she has lined up the blocks of their goose-down
comforter, tugging the sides until they hang
evenly, and lastly smoothing pillows,

tucking corners under the mattress ends
(everyone knows the last turns of making a bed).
When they lay the spray between head- and footstones,
petals resting against new sod, ribbons

falling across where she imagines his chest,
seeing it well done, she frees her heels
from the freshly-watered grass, climbs
in her Lincoln limo and goes.

Dressings

When I saw that I was falling in love
with Death, I felt a rush of relief,
a breasts-to-cheeks blush—
My whole heart turned.

For years I had longed after His
accoutrements: engraved marble, black
letters rippling like a cold stream,
satin ribbons emblazoned with glittered farewells.

Those tiny plexiglass tombs,
photographs of babies, postal badges,
purple hearts, VFW medals, those
I would have stolen for my own living room.

When Death wrapped His hands around
my father's neck until they both purpled—
Death's limpid eyes affirming the love
my father sought—it was a private affair.

When someone asked if I wanted the rosary
curled black around his hands,
I couldn't decide. I didn't know he and Death
had stolen away with only each other.

What's left in the oak box is like the eyeglasses
you see everywhere and admire, the slang phrase you
pick up and hear yourself using, the movie
you go to see alone—not your type—then

one day you understand that these
are the dressings of your next love,
and they fall away like dried petals and, stunned,
you realize your love and know it for its all-alongness,
like letters surfacing in stone.

It's like that now for me and Death. At night
I feel how His body will curl around mine,
I know how tenderly His fingers will touch
the nape of my neck, how naked we leave
the particulars of this world.

III

Before Ash Wednesday

Because I wanted you
naked as sackcloth,
but not in grief, not in ashes,
because I wanted to grow fat on you,
feast with you before the long fast,
because the sky behind the sparkling
float was darkly clear,
we left the reviewing stand, the royal
revelers, jazz bands beating deep
against my walls, dragged your tux,
my taffeta skirt and a thousand
translucent beads and splashes
of doubloons down St. Charles, Napoleon,
until they collapsed across the floor
of your parents' house. Because
I wanted your children and your children's
children, I pretended the eggs were
rushing down like confetti. We could be
anything tonight. I pulled you in,
swallowed you, and your angry father,
your Quarter whore lover and your third grade rape,
I took them all in, as if inside *me*
they might let you go,
small, shriveled newborn in the space heater's glow,
our parting skin slicked red.

Invisible but for the Sun

What I waited for, near that cow pasture
    under a black sky and wary
moon, passed undetected above my head—
    indistinguishable from
the comet. In my sleep I reach back
    for that moment I couldn't see.
I hadn't set out a camera to film

The dead rise from their plaster tombs.
    I didn't set out to prove
the Parousía (to whom?). In light rain,
    fog resting like clouds across hay drifts—
I watched for a long and metallic flame
    I should live to see return.
Prophecy's hard wind blew itself out,

Language ceased, knowledge fell away, silent,
    like long dead stars. The moment was
full, black around the small glowing ribbon
    of our omission. Now look how
radiantly we wait and measure time.
    We might never be closer
than on that night in that clammy pasture:

Next to me was a blond boy I loved who
    said nothing. After many hours,
he held my hand in his square, coarse palm,
    and we stared up at the whole sky.
Somewhere in the comet's womb, a heart
    of black ice, invisible
but for the sun, measures the span of a sky

And moves on. The moment blows a ragged hole
    through a window screen.
We slide from our lawn chairs into the thick
    grass—or so I imagine from
the blackened view. Once unimaginable,
    that flight is now plain absence,
rubbed free from the mind's slated sky.

Eggs and Oranges

Out on the roof we are
thinking about what we haven't said
and eating breakfast. Above,
a blue jay sits alert in the bony black walnut,
mottled by clustered pecans.

Inside, slatted sunlight pierces wet
latex (the warm wine rings and trailing
sheets of *our* generation) beside the bed.
We will not live years together,
share our sleep, live a new language

And learn it. We will not anticipate
each other's steps when we dance, know
where the misplaced object might be found.
We will have eggs and oranges,
chives and toasted wheat—swirls of rye—

Low-nicotine and no-tar cigarettes
out on the roof this morning
this fast ended
this fast.

A Life Without Worry

At any moment a bird might crash
her skull against a tree or against
our sliding glass door, the pane
streak-free, therefore deadly.
I can't imagine a life without worry,

and so I fear heaven and its intractable
bliss, the resulting loss of mind.
It's 102° before noon, although at three
this morning thunderstorms
barged in and I ran from window

to window closing out the rain.
On the Gulf summer storms
seldom bother the heat, which
soon resumes its steam.
But we are not on the Gulf,

and the tow of clouds surprised me.
That we woke together
surprised me, too. Perhaps you had
begun to worry as well. Perhaps
you were already awake, one arm

under your head, annoyed by the heat,
the clock's red glow and my
restless breathing. What saves us
is our partnered sleep. At any moment
our faces might join in abandon.

In the Garden

There we are in the Garden:
she a stone's throw away—
my back to fruit trees—
I watch her
    and touch my side.

None of *my* ribs are missing.
    Her body is her own.

How shrewd the Yahwist,
joining the first lovers with flesh,

with the fierceness

of self-love: the creature craves
a lost bone and tumbles right out of Paradise.

In our Garden
the Snake speaks to both of us,

of course. I follow no one
and eat from my own desire.

And when my gaze wanders off
her breasts,
    green eyes,
        onto an enticing glass pool—

this is Shame.

The Long Wait for the Angel

> *The wait's begun again,*
> *the long wait for the angel,*
> *for that rare, random descent*
> — Sylvia Plath

As a child, I thought the river
was made-up. Hard as I tried to be tall,
pushing against the armrest, lifted higher,

I could see only the levee's grassy wall
encircling nothing beyond the treeline—
no mighty mud stream, no barges, no raft. All

morning they drove the endless green
border. It wasn't the first time they'd lied.
I figured I was a kid who had seen

blue skies called gray; fear shrugged off as pride.
But maybe the water *did* wait there, exhausted,
frightened, and something about me made it hide.

I don't remember when we finally crossed
the Huey Long—the slight jag, twisted,
where east and west momentarily lost

each other, unnaturally grafted
with steel. Below, a brown cover, so flat and wide,
like raw pudding. Neither of us scared.

Now, when this woman says, "I want you inside
me—can't get you out of my head," that fever,
unloved, drowns in the Mississippi's tide.

Margin Lines

You can't drive this far
in my hometown without crossing water.
Southern Missouri is dry and still.
The leaves and deer are frozen quiet.
Trees stand thin as margin lines
against the open spaces.

Your uncle plays his mandolin
for you. He looks down at his boots,
waits for your smile. You hear
every high note as another attack:
no kids, no husband. *You* live in the city.

Your eyes keep so many tears
before you let them fall.
In the graveyard your sobs travel
for miles through barbed wire fences.
You want the dead
to hold you, but they cannot.

You carry antique jars—half-buried
in dirt—from your grandmother's barn
each time you visit the old house.
Across three states they rattle
beneath the car seat, like the chains
of a cartoon ghost. When you rinse them
back home, you see them dissolve
with the muddy dirt.
You can bring nothing there here.

Listen, you are their lovely fawn!
They would feed you skinned apples.
They would watch over you forever.

Distances

The moon again through the window,
like a corner not quite turned.

The distance between
one wall and the other
is the same when I pace
east as when I pace west.
For company
I have driving times and mileage scales,
twining lines of even-numbered
routes running east to west.
Tonight
the only even number of interest
to me is two.

Tonight I am not a passenger, I belong
to the destination. It's a lot harder
to be a landmark. No illusion
of progress. The moon and I just wait.
The clock and I are odometers,
ticking away the distances. And the
permanent distance is desire, which
never fails to add up
to neutral ground, an exit closed,
more construction ahead.
My eyes are caught in the moon,
and the stars, they swerve to avoid me
like day-old road kill.

I feel you coming home to me.

Red Planet

Baja, Mexico

From Mulege you can see Mars's
crimson cloud cascade—
more inviting than the veil-white
calling of Venus, a penlight
on this circus's center ring.
I imagine someone like me
on the other side, watching.

Look, we are told, *but don't consume.*
What are we able to see alone?
My lover has already disappeared
into the mammoth boulders.
Another woman offers me
her pursed lips. She dances
like the naked child everyone ignores.

Is this what it means
to become one? So that parting,
for a time, is like the stomach halved,
open and vulnerable, so used to being full
it is awed by its own grumbling? So that

my lover appears to me
in the wreaths and iron crosses
that line the highway—for those
who didn't make the curve,
went over the side and who I saw, just now,
picking sure red stones among the boulders?

Even for an Afternoon

Irazú, Costa Rica

Outside the unbroached fence,
stretched against hot pavement, lies an enormous cow
    you praise. Half a dozen more
lounge, similarly enlightened, along the narrow
    road we take up the volcano.
Walls ringed like trees, Irazú circles itself
    in a fecund tide.
In its highest crater waits a tranquil lake,
    eerie green, and alert.
I might throw myself down in worship, if not
    for the guardrails, though no doubt
it's you this sleeping ancient wants. Porous rocks
    press against us, chanting.
Even for an afternoon I would not give you
    up to appease some god,
to fill his mouth with the body you offered me—
    kisses you gave last night.
How quickly cloud shadows pass over us.

The Maker's Mark

Old Cemetery, Trujillo, Honduras

Inside these bunker walls almost nothing
Remains of death: granite scarred by lizard claws,
Tradewinds, relentless vines, quivering wrought iron
Stamped with its maker's mark—304 Rampart,
New Orleans. My past always finds me—

Even here—hanging onto the rails
Beside orange tendrils of morning glory.
An iron gate, barely standing—low and wide—
Has frozen open, as if anyone could enter.
Inside the cracked stone, my father

Drops his chin on his chest,
Sighs and sleeps—or is that me, mind
Ablaze, even in death unwilling
To quiet? Then nothing, a fragile sheet of slate.
How far the fleur-de-lis has come

To claim for me what's left of these dead.
A few shards of granite, half a name, a date.
What lives here overwhelms us both—
The fat walls can hardly contain it.
Shore grass and weeds gobble everything

Like the green weave binding Whitman's grave.
Only what dies in the living is truly dead:
The captive spider monkey's touch,
A lizard hiding under trash in broken tombs,
My father's reposed face.

Most Nights

Most nights I try to remember my dreams.
I think of picking blackberries,
plastic buckets full of choice black clusters
and no bugs. Smallish white and pink
berries draped along the barbed wire
beside ant piles and wind-blown shade. The nights here
aren't that clear. There's the light from the streetlamps,
the Harleys racing by, the screeches and
gear shifts in my own mind.

Most nights I try to remember my dreams.
Forget Freud, forget Jung. Forgetting is
the hardest part of sleeping, and sleeping
is the choicest berry on my timeline.
Once I launched half a milk carton
in a swollen ditch with a message for the world:
Drink Kleinpeter's and be happier.
I thought it said, *I am alone*
on a crowded Southern island. Come soon.

Hell, Late Twentieth Century

after Canto XI, Dante's Inferno

In the second ring, called despondence,
we sit cross-legged and turn our gloomy
hearts on a spit. The change is luminous:

we find figures of joy in blue flames,
hold the forearms we'd scarred to our chests
and count embers like falling grains.

When ice flows to reverse
our pain, we breathe in cool fog
until our flesh grays. It could be worse.

Memories of the lost world surface
as palm-shaped bruises on cheekbones:
beaches we walked, steely and gazeless,

bright fruit we ignored or ate with no taste,
sharp winter days we groped past, or slept
through, and that retriever who chased

us from bed to bath, carrying
ball then bone in adoration—we reach
into yellow vapor, touch nothing,
and scratch the air of her head and ears.

Conversion

The tracks got ripped up like a busted zipper,
thrown down, piles of tar and broken ties,
into the dead grass on the bayouside.

You have to understand: only time tears things
down here. Long after you quit a house, pack
up and leave, that house stands

Catalogued, under sheets of rust, paneless,
porchless, for years. Cast-iron kettles
won't move, won't be moved,

The air above their bellies, still and sharp.
No one remembers the cane they boiled
or how they came to kill grass

Where they do. Half an old bridge
makes a sweet fishing spot—but taking
the rails away, it was an insult, really,

A theft. I saw how one loss collapses
into another, the rings between them,
almost indistinguishable.

But then, to the right of the road,
the shoulder leapt with sunflowers,
the blue sky dangled like a scarf,

And the part of me that was buried
came back like the dead after hard rain,
just pushed up the glass lid

And stepped onto solid ground. Backwater rises
to its own schedule, covers the highways,
you can't tell the bayou's banks

From the road's edge, and then there's no question
of staving off conversion.
Even the dead won't be held down.

Finishing Touch

Ever since the painter depicted
Your finger extended to Your creature,

we have known we crave a surrogate touch.
We press others' palms to our faces,

as if we were still being molded,
polished by an apprenticed love revising

our rougher destinies: Each hand found
more skillful than the last, each imprint closer

to Your transforming seal. I know this,
and still I have to ask for reprieve

in illusion, to linger in this present
flesh, believe in her finishing touch.

I want *this* hand: its knowing strokes
inside my thighs where all portrayal begins.

Let this hand complete me for the stretch,
the soft edges of these fingers be the last

of earth I feel, let it be her own
hand—hers alone—that will close these eyes.

Notes

"As If There Were Only One" is for Harold Bloom.

"*La Toussaint*, 1944" is for Jo Ann Cangemi.

The italicized statement in "Red Planet" paraphrases Simone Weil.

"Hell, Late Twentieth Century" takes as its origin the *Inferno*, XI. 42-6, Singleton translation:

> A man may lay violent hand upon himself, and upon his own property; and therefore in the second ring must every one repent in vain who deprives himself of your world, gambles and dissipates his substance, and weeps there where he should be joyous.

"Finishing Touch" is for Audrey Colombe.

photo by Audrey Colombe

Martha Serpas is a native of Galliano, Louisiana, and a graduate
of Louisiana State University, New York University, Yale Divinity
School, and the University of Houston. Her poems are included
in *Uncommonplace: An Anthology of Louisiana Poets* (LSU Press).
She has led writing workshops for children and teachers in
schools, shelters, and juvenile facilities. A frequent lecturer on
poetry and belief, she teaches at the University of Tampa.

Harold Bloom is Sterling Professor of the Humanities at Yale
University, Berg Professor of English at New York University,
and a past Charles Eliot Norton professor at Harvard University.
His most recent works include *How to Read and Why* (Scribner,
2000), the best-selling *Shakespeare: The Invention of the Human*
(Riverhead, 1999), and *The Western Canon: The Books and School
of the Ages* (Harcourt Brace, 1994). The author of more than
twenty books, including *The Anxiety of Influence,* he is a member
of the American Academy of Arts and Letters, where in 1999
he was awarded the Gold Medal for belles lettres and criticism.
Among many other awards and honorary degrees, he has
received a MacArthur Prize Fellowship.

New Issues Poetry & Prose

Editor, Herbert Scott

James Armstrong, *Monument In A Summer Hat*
Michael Burkard, *Pennsylvania Collection Agency*
Anthony Butts, *Fifth Season*
Kevin Cantwell, *Something Black in the Green Part of Your Eye*
Gladys Cardiff, *A Bare Unpainted Table*
Kevin Clark, *In the Evening of No Warning*
Jim Daniels, *Night with Drive-By Shooting Stars*
Joseph Featherstone, *Brace's Cove*
Lisa Fishman, *The Deep Heart's Core Is a Suitcase*
Robert Grunst, *The Smallest Bird in North America*
Mark Halperin, *Time as Distance*
Myronn Hardy, *Approaching the Center*
Edward Haworth Hoeppner, *Rain Through High Windows*
Cynthia Hogue, *Flux*
Janet Kauffman, *Rot* (fiction)
Josie Kearns, *New Numbers*
Maurice Kilwein Guevara, *Autobiography of So-and-so: Poems in Prose*
Ruth Ellen Kocher, *When the Moon Knows You're Wandering*
Steve Langan, *Freezing*
Lance Larsen, *Erasable Walls*
David Dodd Lee, *Downsides of Fish Culture*
Deanne Lundin, *The Ginseng Hunter's Notebook*
Joy Manesiotis, *They Sing to Her Bones*
Sarah Mangold, *Household Mechanics*
David Marlatt, *A Hog Slaughtering Woman*
Paula McLain, *Less of Her*
Sarah Messer, *Bandit Letters*
Malena Mörling, *Ocean Avenue*
Julie Moulds, *The Woman with a Cubed Head*
Marsha de la O, *Black Hope*
C. Mikal Oness, *Water Becomes Bone*
Elizabeth Powell, *The Republic of Self*
Margaret Rabb, *Granite Dives*
Rebecca Reynolds, *Daughter of the Hangnail*
Martha Rhodes, *Perfect Disappearance*
Beth Roberts, *Brief Moral History in Blue*